DISCOVER!

AMERICA'S AMAZING LANDMARKS

THE LINCOLN MEMORIAL

By Marie Roesser

Enslow PUBLISHING

Please visit our website, www.enslow.com. For a free color catalog of all our high-quality books, call toll free 1-800-398-2504 or fax 1-877-980-4454.

Library of Congress Cataloging-in-Publication Data
Names: Roesser, Marie, author.
Title: The Lincoln Memorial / Marie Roesser.
Description: New York : Enslow Publishing, [2026] | Series: America's amazing landmarks | Includes index.
Identifiers: LCCN 2024059903 (print) | LCCN 2024059904 (ebook) | ISBN 9781978544048 (lib. bdg.) | ISBN 9781978544031 (paperback) | ISBN 9781978544055 (ebook)
Subjects: LCSH: Lincoln Memorial (Washington, D.C.)–Juvenile literature.
Classification: LCC F203.4.L73 R64 2026 (print) | LCC F203.4.L73 (ebook) | DDC 975.3–dc23/eng/20250214
LC record available at https://lccn.loc.gov/2024059903
LC ebook record available at https://lccn.loc.gov/2024059904

Portions of this work were originally authored by Audrey Erin and published as *Visit the Lincoln Memorial.* All new material this edition authored by Marie Roesser.

Published in 2026 by
Enslow Publishing
2544 Clinton Street
Buffalo, NY 14224

Cover Designer: Nicholas Switalski
Interior Designer: Rachel Rising
Editor: Therese Shea

Photo credits: Cover, p. 1 Kamira/Shutterstock.com; Cover, pp.1, 3-24 Jeffery Edwards/Shutterstock.com; pp. 1, 5, 7, 9, 11, 13, 15, 19, 21 Oleksandr Poliashenko/Shutterstock.com; p. 4 Wangkun Jia/Shutterstock.com; p. 5 Peter Hermes Furian/Shutterstock.com; p. 7 https://en.m.wikipedia.org/wiki/File:Mary_Todd_Lincoln_1846-1847_restored.png; p. 7 https://en.m.wikipedia.org/wiki/File:Abraham_Lincoln_by_Nicholas_Shepherd,_1846-crop.jpg; p. 9 https://commons.wikimedia.org/wiki/File:Maryland,_Antietam,_President_Lincoln_on_the_Battlefield_-_NARA_-_533297.jpg; p.10 https://commons.wikimedia.org/wiki/File:John_Wilkes_Booth-portrait.jpg; p. 11 https://commons.wikimedia.org/wiki/File:Lincoln_assassination_slide_c1900_-_Restoration.jpg; p. 13 christianthiel.net/Shutterstock.com; p. 15 Sean Pavone/Shutterstock.com; p. 17 ChicagoPhotographer/Shutterstock.com; p. 17 Brian Logan Photography/Shutterstock.com; p. 19 Sergii Figurnyi/Shutterstock.com; p. 21 S.Borisov/Shutterstock.com.

Printed in the United States of America

Some of the images in this book illustrate individuals who are models. The depictions do not imply actual situations or events.

CPSIA compliance information: Batch #CSENS26: For further information contact Enslow Publishing, at 1-800-398-2504.

CONTENTS

BOLDFACE WORDS APPEAR IN THE GLOSSARY.

LINCOLN'S LEGACY

Abraham Lincoln remains one of the most respected U.S. presidents more than 150 years after his death. Each year, millions of people learn more about his life and **legacy** by visiting the Lincoln Memorial in Washington, D.C.

Lincoln Memorial

A MEMORIAL IS AN OBJECT BUILT TO HONOR A PERSON OR EVENT.

YOUNG LINCOLN

Lincoln was born in Kentucky on February 12, 1809. His family moved to Indiana and then Illinois. He didn't go to school much. His mother taught him to read. Lincoln became a **lawyer** and an Illinois **legislator**. He ran for U.S. Senate in 1858 but lost.

Abraham Lincoln, 1846

Mary Todd Lincoln

LINCOLN MARRIED MARY TODD IN 1842. THEY HAD FOUR SONS.

PRESIDENT LINCOLN

Lincoln ran for U.S. president in 1860. He won. The country was **divided** over slavery at that time. When Lincoln won, many Southern states broke away from the rest of the United States. A **civil war** was fought between the North and South from 1861 to 1865.

THE SOUTHERN STATES FORMED THE CONFEDERATE STATES OF AMERICA. THE REST OF THE COUNTRY REMAINED PART OF THE UNITED STATES AND WERE SOMETIMES CALLED THE UNION.

ASSASSINATION

The Union won the American Civil War. Slavery was soon ended. On April 14, 1865, Lincoln was assassinated, or killed, as he watched a play. He died the next day. Many people wanted to honor Lincoln with a memorial.

John Wilkes Booth

LINCOLN WAS SHOT BY AN ACTOR NAMED JOHN WILKES BOOTH.

MANY YEARS IN THE MAKING

In 1867, Congress created a group to plan a memorial for Lincoln. However, that monument was never built. In 1900, the park called the National Mall was **designed** in Washington, D.C. A memorial for Lincoln was planned on the western end of the mall.

THE NATIONAL MALL IS A LONG PARK THAT CONTAINS MANY MONUMENTS, MUSEUMS, MEMORIALS, AND OTHER IMPORTANT BUILDINGS.

ON THE RIVER

The Lincoln Memorial is on the Potomac River for a reason. This river was the dividing line between the North and South during the American Civil War. But Lincoln brought the two sides together again. Lincoln's memorial was built with stones from Northern and Southern states.

THE LINCOLN MEMORIAL WAS BUILT BETWEEN 1914 AND 1922.

OUTSIDE AND INSIDE

Architect Henry Bacon designed the Lincoln Memorial to look like the Parthenon, an old Greek building. Thirty-six **columns** surround the memorial because there were 36 U.S. states in 1865. There are three chambers, or rooms, inside. Two chambers display, or show, two of Lincoln's most famous speeches.

Gettysburg Address

Second Inaugural Address

LINCOLN'S STATUE

A statue of Abraham Lincoln is in the middle chamber. **Sculptor** Daniel Chester French wanted to show Lincoln's kindness and strength. He sculpted one of Lincoln's hands closed in a fist, showing his strength. The other hand is more open, showing his kindness.

LINCOLN'S STATUE IS 19 FEET (5.8 M) HIGH AND 19 FEET WIDE.

VISIT THE MEMORIAL

People can visit the Lincoln Memorial any time of day and any day of the year. National Park Service workers take care of the memorial and the rest of the National Mall. They also answer visitors' questions. Visitors can learn many more facts about the memorial and the man it honors.

THE STEPS OF THE LINCOLN MEMORIAL HAVE BEEN THE LOCATION OF FAMOUS EVENTS, INCLUDING MARTIN LUTHER KING JR.'S "I HAVE A DREAM" SPEECH.

GLOSSARY

architect: A person who designs, or plans, buildings.

civil war: A war between two groups within a country.

column: A tall, strong supporting post.

design: To create the pattern or shape of something.

divide: To break up.

lawyer: Someone whose job it is to help people with their questions and problems with the law.

legacy: Something that is passed down from someone.

legislator: A member of a lawmaking body of government.

museum: A building in which things of interest are displayed.

sculptor: An artist who creates a shape with stone, wood, metal, or other matter.

FOR MORE INFORMATION

Books

Carr, Aaron. *Lincoln Memorial.* New York, NY: Lightbox Learning Inc., 2023.

London, Martha. *Abraham Lincoln.* Focus Readers, MN: Lake Elmo, 2023.

Websites

Abraham Lincoln
kids.britannica.com/students/article/Abraham-Lincoln/275480
Read more about Lincoln's life and leadership.

Lincoln Memorial
www.nps.gov/linc/
Check out the official website of the Lincoln Memorial and plan a visit.

Publisher's note to educators and parents: Our editors have carefully reviewed these websites to ensure that they are suitable for students. Many websites change frequently, however, and we cannot guarantee that a site's future contents will continue to meet our high standards of quality and educational value. Be advised that students should be closely supervised whenever they access the internet.

INDEX